IN THE TARTAN SOCKS

by Susan Cohen
Illustrated by Dasha Zeleno

www.theweebookcompany.com

A catalogue record of this book is available from the British Library.

ISBN: 9781913237455

Printed in Scotland by Bell & Bain Ltd, Glasgow

THE WEE BOOK COMPANY
wee books with big voices

‘DON’T YOU KNOW YET?
IT IS YOUR LIGHT THAT LIGHTS THE WORLD.’

Rumi

Jock the fox in the tartan socks was a creature of the night. He slept when the sun was up and roamed when the moon was out. It was all he'd ever known.

To him, the night was home.

Yet there were times when even Jock felt overwhelmed by the darkness. Sometimes it was so hard ducking and diving, only just surviving. Sometimes it was so hard to keep trying, trying, trying to find his way.

Surely there had to be another way?

One day Jock realised he had to make a change.
He decided to make a different choice.

In his low fox voice he said to himself, ‘even though I belong to the night, I am going to break free and seek out the light. When the early morning sun starts to shine bright, I’m going to climb higher than high and sit under the big blue sky.’

And so he did.

He climbed

and climbed

and climbed ...

... until he reached the very top of the highest hill,
where the air was clear and oh-so still.

'Wow!' he said, 'I can see for miles. So this
is what my world has looked like all the while.'

Jock sat and looked and b-r-e-a-t-h-e-d. He was so happy to quietly just be.

Slowly, slowly he started to feel the light deep in his heart.

In time, the sun started falling and night started calling.

By sunset's glow, Jock knew it was time for him to go.

Safely home, Jock was surrounded by darkness but something felt different. Jock now had light in his heart – and all because he had made a different choice.

In his low fox voice, he said to himself, 'it is not enough to simply survive. I am going to live! I am going to thrive!'

And so he did.

Pippa McGatt the tiny wee bat was hanging around. In the starry stillness, when there is no sound, she sometimes feels a little lost, she sometimes feels a little down.

Roger McCadger the big-hearted badger stepped out of the trees. On his night-time wanders, there are times when he ponders how hard it can be to live in the dark.

Lorna McCowell the clever night owl perched on a fence, feeling a little tired, a little tense. On her night flights, she sometimes wonders if life could just be a wee bit ... well ... easier.

That night, through the darkness, they all sensed something different – a faint glimmer, an ever-so-slight shimmer, a soft low gentle glow.

'Wow!' they thought, 'whatever can that be?'

They really didn't know.

Jock looked different.

‘Wow!’ they said to Jock, ‘whatever happened to you?’

Jock’s heart was full. He smiled at his friends.

‘Well, whatever it is,’ they said, ‘can you help it to happen to us too?’

Jock nodded.

‘Of course!’ he said, ‘come with me – you’ll see!’

And so they did.

Just as the early morning sun started to shine bright
Jock the fox in the tartan socks
Pippa McGatt the tiny wee bat
Roger McCadger the big-hearted badger
and
Lorna McCowell the clever night owl

climbed

and climbed

and climbed ...

... until they reached the very top of the highest hill.

'Wow!' they said, 'just wow!'

In time, the sun started falling and night started calling.

By sunset's glow, the friends knew it was time for them to go.

Safely home, they were surrounded by darkness but something was different, something had changed and nothing would ever be the same again.

The friends could see that they had discovered another way to be. Their inner lights shone, all shadows of sadness gone.

It was as if their hearts held the strength of the sun.

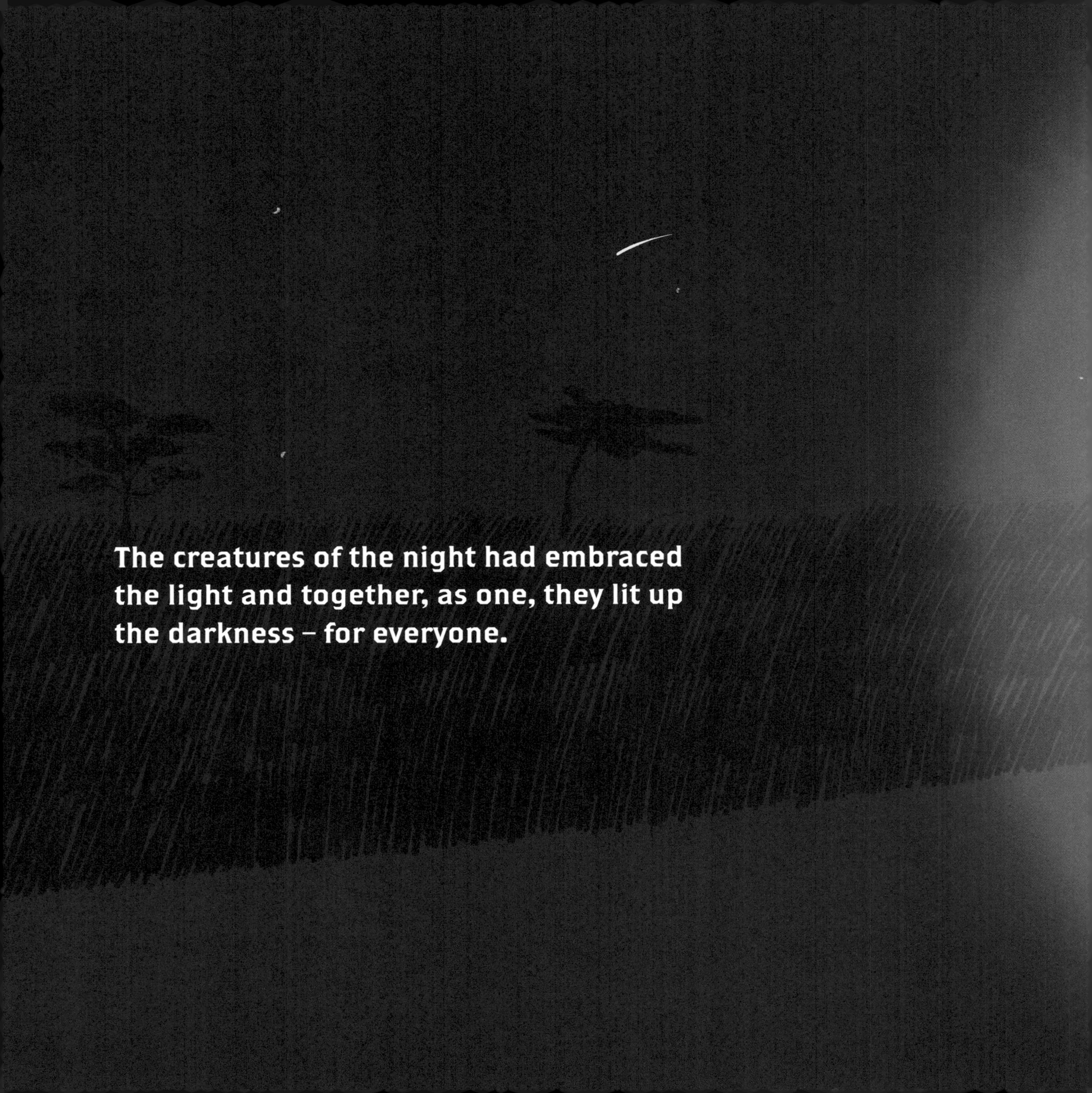

The creatures of the night had embraced the light and together, as one, they lit up the darkness – for everyone.

Also from The Wee Book Company ...

Bea and Brodie's Mindful Journey
Bea and Brodie's Magical Journey
Nessie's Secret, About Being One Of A Kind
Nessie and Me, About The Power Of The Mind
Wee Deoch an Doris
Stop Yer Ticklin Jock!
Here They Come! The Scottish Pipes an Drums
Here They Come! The Scottish Highland Games
Callum & Cullen – In The Same Boat, An Island Adventure

and more ...

MIX
Paper from responsible sources
FSC® C007785